EXTREME SPORTS

Barbara C. Bourassa

Library of Congress Control Number: 2007000931

ISBN 978-1-59566-347-4

Written by Barbara C. Bourassa
Edited, designed and picture researched by
    Starry Dog Books Ltd
Consultant Steven Downes, of the Sports Journalists'
    Association www.sportsjournalists.co.uk

Publisher Steve Evans
Creative Director Zeta Davies
Senior Editor Hannah Ray

Printed and bound in China

Web site information is correct at time of going to press. However, the publishers cannot accept liability for any information or links found on third-party Web sites.

All the sports in this book involve varying degrees of difficulty and the publisher would strongly advise that none of the activities mentioned is undertaken without adult supervision or the guidance of a professional coach.

Words in **bold** can be found in the Glossary on pages 30–31.

S = Shutterstock.com, C = Corbis,
D = Dreamstime.com, G = Getty Images,
BSP = Big Stock Photo.com,
ISP = iStockphoto.com, F = Fotolia.com

t = top, b = bottom, l = left, r = right, c = centre, FC = front cover, BC = back cover

FC (main image) G/ © Philip & Karen Smith, (top to bottom) ISP/ © Brent Deuel, D/ © Isoft123, D/ © Partyof7infl, courtesy of the National Dutch Scooter (Footbike) Federation, F/ © Jarvis Gray, F/ © Eric Foltz, F/ © Nicholas Rjabow. BC D/ © Ijansempoi.

1 D/ © Ijansempoi; 4 S/ © Putchenko Kirill Victorovich; 5 (top to bottom) F/ © Jarvis Gray, F/ © Eric Foltz, F/ © Nicholas Rjabow, F/ © dogbone66; 6t C/ © Elmar Krenkel/Zefa, 6b C/ © Martin Philbey/ZUMA; 7 (main image) C/ © Al Fuchs/NewSport; 8b courtesy of the National Dutch Scooter (Footbike) Federation; 9t D/ © Vangelis; 9b C/ © LWA- JDC; 10b G/ © Ryan McVay; 11t G/ © Michael Kelley; 11 (main image) D/ © Kineticimagery; 12t (left to right) S/ © Peter Weber, S/ © Shawn Pecor, S/ © Byron W.Moore; 12b S/ © Lavigne Herve; 13 (main image) G/ © Philip & Karen Smith, 13b courtesy of IMBA-UK; 14b D/ © Godfer; 15t S/ © Nick Poling, 15b C/ © Stuart Westmorland; 16–17 courtesy of Gomberg Kites; 17t G/ © Karl Weatherly; 18t G/ © Jump Run Productions, 18b © Drew Brophy; 19 G/ © Warren Bolster; 20t courtesy of Connelly Skis; 20b C/ © Elizabeth Kreutz/NewSport; 21t ISP/ © James Boulette, 21 (main image) ISP/ © Brent Deuel; 22t C/ © Nawang Sherpa/Bogati/ZUMA, 22b G/ © Zigy Kaluzny; 23 G/ © Ryan McVay; 24b C/ © James L. Amos; 25t C/ © Ariel Skelley; 25b D/ © Isoft123; 26 courtesy of Teresa Nightingale, www.attentiondesign.ca; 27l F/ © Serge Simo, 27r © Meghan Lapeta; 28t courtesy of www.usaswimming.org/ Sara McLarty and family, 28b G/ © David Madison; 29 G/ Mike Powell.

CONTENTS

INTRODUCTION

THE TERM "extreme sport" means many things to many people. For children, however, it usually means cutting-edge sports such as skateboarding, surfing, IronKids (**triathlon**), and mountain biking. The term became widely used beginning in 1995, when the sports channel ESPN launched the Extreme Games (later changed to the **X Games**), an international competition for more unusual, exciting sports.

Trendy, but not new!

Most of the extreme sports in this book have a modern reputation, but some have been around for a very long time. Surfing and kiting, for example, are actually thousands of years old. Rock climbing dates back to the 1880s, while mountain biking and kneeboarding are child-friendly versions of adult sports (motocross/BMX and waterskiing).

▶ *Rock climbing is a little like learning to ride a bike because once you have learned the basics, you'll never forget them!*

PROTECTIVE GEAR

You'll notice that people who you see climbing vertical rock faces, performing "ollies" in a skate park, or kayaking down rushing rivers always wear protective gear. You'll usually see them with a helmet, pads, ropes, life jackets, and the like. The right gear is important because many extreme sports lift you into the air, and wearing protection around your head and body can prevent injuries when you come back down to Earth. As the proverb says, "What goes up, must come down!"

Learning the basics

As any good **coach** will tell you, learning a new sport means understanding and mastering the basics. You'll need to take good care of your equipment, practice a lot, and make sure you have expert help. All sports keep you healthy and active. So remember to drink plenty of water, eat well, and take breaks whenever you need to, whether you're running a race, riding a trail, or kayaking down a river.

Stay safe

Photographs of extreme sports are often exciting and fun to look at, but the people pictured are usually very experienced and have practiced for years. They may also be using expensive, specialized equipment. Don't expect to be able to perform the same moves right away. However, you can expect to have a fun and exciting time if you put safety first—so turn the page to get the lowdown on a range of awesome extreme sports!

SKATEBOARDING dates back to the 1950s. Many sports experts say that skateboarding originated in California, where the sport of surfing met the sport of roller-skating. This resulted in the invention of a long, flat board with four wheels attached—the skateboard! To get a skateboard moving, you stand on it with one foot and push it along with the other. Once you have some speed, you glide along with both feet on the board.

FIX IT YOURSELF!

Many people repair their own skateboards using special tools. The wheels of a skateboard sometimes wear out, and the surface of the board may need repainting with a fresh new design.

What's an "ollie"?

An "ollie" is a common skateboarding move in which the skateboarder steps down on the back of the board in order to lift up the front and "get air." It is named after Alan "Ollie" Gelfand, a world-famous skateboarder from California.

◀ Skateboarders often wear specially designed shoes with shock-absorbing heel pads and flat rubber soles that grip the board well.

THE RIGHT GEAR

When you are skateboarding, you should always wear a helmet and knee and elbow pads for protection.

Pro skater girl!

Elissa Streamer has won three gold medals in women's street skate at the X Games. She started skateboarding at the age of 12.

WORLD'S LONGEST RAMP JUMP

According to the Guinness Book of World Records, the longest skateboard ramp jump was performed by professional skateboarder Danny Way at the 2004 X Games in Los Angeles, California. Way jumped an astonishing 78.7 feet (24m)!

▲ *Wagner Ramos is a professional skateboarder, which means he skates for money, not just for fun!*

Skateboard dude

Wagner Ramos, a 16-year-old skateboarder from Brazil, was chosen as best all-round athlete at the 2006 **Gravity Games**. Friends describe him as a "mellow fellow" who loves music.

SCOOTING

A SCOOTER is a close relative of the skateboard. It is essentially a skateboard with a long handle and two narrow wheels similar to rollerblade wheels. Razor scooters got their name because they resemble an old-fashioned barber's razor—the kind with a blade that flips out from a long handle.

Mopeds and foot bikes

"Scooter" is also a term for a moped—a two-wheeled, motorcycle-like vehicle popular in Italy. Mopeds are ideal for getting around narrow city streets. Another kind of scooter is the foot bike—a bicycle with a flat, scooter-like platform in the center. The rider pushes the bike along with one foot.

HOW TO RIDE A RAZOR SCOOTER

To ride a razor scooter, place one foot on the flat part of the scooter and use your other foot to push the scooter along. Alternatively, place your second foot behind the first and glide! Use the T-shaped handle bar to steer.

Motorized scooters

Some motorized scooters look just like razor scooters, but have small engines at the back. Others, called mini scooters, stand just under 3.3 feet (1m) tall and feature T-shaped handlebars. Some people want to ban certain types of motorized scooter because they can travel up to 40 mph (64kph), but offer no protection for the rider if they collide with another vehicle.

Foot bike races take place either on roads or special tracks. Competitors can race for individual medals or as part of a team in relay races.

To stop a razor scooter, use your foot to press down on the brake that extends over the back wheel.

RAZORS AND ROLLERBLADES

A razor scooter has narrow wheels, like those on rollerblades (above). Some scooter riders have learned to be just as agile as rollerbladers, and can perform amazing stunts.

MOUNTAIN BIKING

IF YOU LIKE riding your bike, and you like **hiking** in the woods or along rough tracks, you will probably like mountain biking. Mountain biking is just what it sounds like—riding a special bike up and down hills or mountains. Some people bike in the summer on the same mountains that are used for skiing in the winter. People also bike through woods, across deserts, or on other types of rough **terrain**.

WHERE TO BIKE

Wondering where to mountain bike? Ask your local librarian for information about trails that are open to mountain bikes, or find out where your nearest mountain-biking group meets.

Special gear

Mountain biking requires a special bike—a mountain bike! Mountain bikes have wide, bumpy tires that grip the **trail** and keep the bike stable on rocks, roots, or muddy ground. Like other bikes, mountain bikes also have gears, which let you get more power from the bike (in low gears) or more speed (in higher gears).

▶ *On a smooth road surface, a mountain bike needs more pedal-power to go the same speed as a road bike. This is because its tires provide such good grip that they slow the bike down.*

➡ *Practice is an important part of mountain biking. You'll need to practice braking, especially if you are riding up and down hills or steep slopes.*

SAFETY FIRST

As with many extreme sports, a helmet and knee and elbow pads will protect you from falls or flying rocks. In the extreme version of mountain biking, called **bicycle motocross (BMX)**, participants wear padded suits, protective gloves, goggles, and shoes that grip the pedals. The full-face helmet worn by BMX riders closely resembles those used for skiing, riding motorcycles, or **snowmobiling**.

OLYMPIC GAMES

Cross-country mountain biking was first officially included in the Olympics in 1996. That year, Bart Brentjens of the Netherlands won the gold medal. He also won an Olympic bronze in 2004.

Mt. biking

Be prepared!

Muddy or rocky trails can wear out both you and your bike, so it is important to carry a few essentials with you. Take a water bottle, so you don't get dehydrated, and a repair kit, in case you need to repair your bike in a remote place. Your repair kit should include a multi-tool designed to repair bikes, a patch kit for fixing flat tires, and a small pump.

➤ *In a motocross race, all riders start at the same time, and the first biker across the finish line wins.*

TRIATHLONS

Three-part, multi-sport events are called triathlons. Racing bikes along roads usually forms one part of the race. But some special triathlons, often called XTerras, involve mountain biking instead. Participants swim in a lake, go mountain biking, and then run to the finish.

Motocross and BMX

Motocross is related to mountain biking, but motorcycles are ridden instead of bicycles. The gas-powered motorcycles can go much faster and cover longer distances than mountain bikes. BMX bikes are pedal-powered racing bikes. They have smaller wheels than mountain bikes and are designed for strength.

HOLD TIGHT!

Motocross is very demanding! Riders must control a heavy motorcycle while driving as fast as possible on a rough and bumpy course.

→ *Mountain biking is a great form of exercise. Pedaling uses the muscles in your legs and hips, and steering the bike strengthens your arm muscles.*

Brake power

A mountain bike's brakes (called **cantilever brakes**) are more like motorcycle brakes than a road bike's **caliper brakes**. Cantilever brakes give you more control over how fast you come down a hill. Many experienced mountain bikers descend using a technique called feathering—gently squeezing and releasing the brake repeatedly. Feathering can prevent the wheels from locking. If your wheels lock, you can go into a spin, which could cause an injury.

I·M·B·A
International Mountain Bicycling Association

IMBA

The International Mountain Bicycling Association (IMBA) is dedicated to preserving and expanding trails for mountain biking. Its members ride on trails all over the world. Check it out at: www.imba.com

13

SNORKELING is a fun and easy extreme sport, providing you can swim! All you need to get started is a mask, a snorkel, and flippers. You can snorkel in a fresh lake, exploring the shoreline for tadpoles and frogs, or in the ocean, where you might see brightly colored fish swim by.

FLIPPERS

To swim with flippers, you'll need to learn how to do the "flutter kick." This involves kicking rapidly back and forth with your legs straight (no bending at the knees).

Fun with flippers

Breathing through a snorkel and swimming with a mask and flippers all at the same time may take a little while to learn. If you are a beginner, first try swimming with just the flippers to get used to the feel of them. You'll be able to go really fast!

Mask and snorkel

A snorkeling mask is fun to wear because it lets you see while keeping the water out of your eyes. Breathing through the mouthpiece and the tube of the snorkel takes practice. Don't forget to hold your breath if you dive under the water because water will go down the tube! You will need to blow the water back out of the tube when you come back up to the surface.

◀ The rubber rim of a snorkel mask fits tightly around the face so that water can't get in.

SNORKELING

Scuba diving

Scuba diving is a sport for adults. Wearing special equipment, scuba divers can swim deep under the sea and can stay under water for long periods of time. Sometimes they are hired to look for treasure or shipwrecks.

Diving deep

Scuba divers carry **oxygen tanks** on their backs for underwater breathing and wear wetsuits, rubber gloves, and rubber boots. They may also wear a headlamp because it's very dark deep in the ocean!

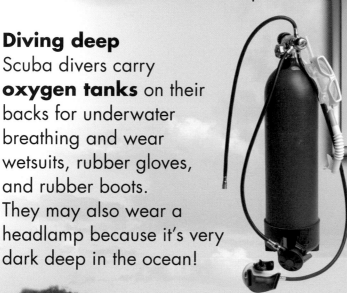

WORLD RECORD

In June 2005, South African scuba diver Nuno Gomes set a new world record in diving. Gomes dived to a depth of 1,044.13 feet (318.25m). That is almost equal to the height of the Eiffel Tower in Paris, France! For more world records, check out: www.guinnessworldrecords.com

➤ In shallow coastal waters, a snorkeler can see all kinds of wonderful things, such as these starfish off the coast of Honeymoon Island, Palau, in the Pacific Ocean.

KITING

WHEN YOU think of kite flying, you may think of a simple diamond-shaped piece of plastic, a few wooden sticks, and a ball of string. But kiting gets far more extreme than that! Competitive kite flying is growing in popularity. In the USA, Germany, Japan, and Thailand (among other countries) people fly giant kites more than 79 feet (24m) in length.

Kite varieties

There are many different types of kites, including single-string kites, which you may have flown in a field or on a beach; stunt kites, which are designed to do tricks or special maneuvers; and power kites, which have enough power to pull surfers across the ocean or **snowboarders** across snow.

STACK

STACK stands for Sport Team and Competitive Kiting, an organization that tries to bring together anyone who loves the sport of kiting. Its members compete in Individual, Pairs, Team, and Trick-flying kite competitions all over the world.

Kiting is often done at the beach. There is plenty of room to run and launch a kite and good wind blowing in off the ocean to lift it.

WORLD'S SMALLEST AND BIGGEST KITES

Kites range from very small to huge. According to the Guinness Book of World Records, the smallest kite ever flown measured 0.4 x 0.3 inches (10 x 8mm)—about the size of a pea. This miniature kite was flown by Nobuhiko Yoshizuni of Kyoto, Japan. In complete contrast, the MegaFlag, produced by a company called Gomberg Kite Productions, measures 131.2 x 78.7 feet (40 x 24m). That's bigger than most houses!

Festivals and competitions

One easy way to become familiar with kiting is to go to a competition or festival. There are kite competitions for speed and design, and festivals that celebrate sport kites, **box kites**, foils (soft, semi-inflated kites used for kitesurfing and **snowkiting**), and deltas (arrow-shaped kites used for stunts). A major kiting event is held each year in Washington, DC. It includes a kite design competition which is judged based on visual appeal and handling, and trick flying competitions.

To kitesurf, you need to be a strong swimmer and a skilled kite-flyer.

Kitesurfing

To kitesurf, you use a large kite to pull yourself across water on a wakeboard Experts are able to perform amazing jumps.

SNOWKITING

Snowkiting is similar to kitesurfing, but instead combines a kite and a snowboard. Check out the Swiss Snowkiting School's Web site: www.snowkiting.ch (To get the English-language version, click on "english" in the black bar at the top of the home page.)

SURFING

SURFING may have its roots in the ancient cultures of Polynesia and Tahiti. It was witnessed in the late 1770s by explorer Captain James Cook. Cook traveled through the Hawaiian islands, where he saw the native people riding waves on wooden boards. Today's boards, made from a special kind of **resin**-coated plastic, include surfboards, paipo (short boards), and round **skimmers**.

Skysurfers wear parachutes on their backs. The chutes carry them safely back to the ground after surfing for a while.

The biggest waves

Major surfing centers have popped up along the Pacific and Atlantic coasts. These coasts have some of the world's biggest waves. Australia, California, and Hawaii all have strong surfing communities. By some estimates, there are 20 million surfers worldwide. The sport is exciting to watch, especially the world-class surfers, who tackle the biggest waves the ocean can produce.

Take to the air

Surfing brings together a body, a board, and a wave. Skysurfing combines a body, a board, and the air. Skysurfers jump out of a plane and ride air currents using a board strapped to their feet! Only highly trained professionals are able to do this sport.

SURF ART

Surfboard artist Drew Brophy of California is extremely well known among musicians. In fact, his painted surfboards sell for thousands of dollars! Drew says his designs are inspired by the ocean, surfing, and nature.

Surfing vs. bodyboarding

Watching the world's best surfers and learning how to surf are two very different things! Learning to surf (or **windsurf**, which adds a sail and apparatus to the board) requires time and patience. You may prefer bodyboarding—surfing while lying down on a 3.3-foot (1m) long board (also called a boogie board). You could also try riding a skimmer—a round, thin board. To ride a skimboard, you run toward the water from the beach. Then you jump on the board with both feet and glide through the shallow water.

WORLD RECORD HOLDER

According to the Guinness Book of World Records, Mike Stewart has won 9 world championships in bodyboarding and 21 Pipeline titles. (Pipeline is a famous Hawaiian wave venue.)

While lying on the board, a surfer first paddles out to sea. When a wave comes in, the surfer stands up on his or her feet. Some surfers prefer to crouch on one knee first to make sure both feet are in the right position before standing.

SURF LINGO

Surfing has a language and culture all its own. In California, for instance, "cooking" means a great wave and "noodled" means exhausted. "Wipe out" means to fall off the board, which is when you don't want to meet a "landlord" (a great white shark). "Hang ten" refers to a move in which you have all ten toes on the nose (front) of the board.

KNEEBOARDING

KNEEBOARDING and wakeboarding are great extreme water sports. These sports require the proper equipment: a good teacher, a snug life jacket, and a powerboat. When kneeboarding, you are pulled behind a boat while kneeling on a board. When wakeboarding, you are also pulled behind a boat, but you stand sideways on a board resembling a snowboard.

◀ Wakeboards have to be very strong. They have to withstand pounding as their riders jump over the waves created behind the boat.

Waterskiing

Both kneeboarding and wakeboarding are related to waterskiing, in which you are pulled behind a powerboat while standing on wide, flat skis. Waterskiing has a long history and is an Olympic sport. Check it out at www.usawaterski.org

Barefooting

Barefoot waterskiing involves skiing on water using your bare feet! At the 2006 Barefoot Water Ski World Championships, Keith St. Onge won the Men's **Slalom**, Tricks, and Overall categories. He started waterskiing at the age of 10 and has had years of experience, so don't try any of his tricks at home!

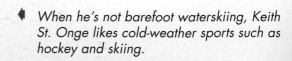

◀ When he's not barefoot waterskiing, Keith St. Onge likes cold-weather sports such as hockey and skiing.

Many people find kneeboarding easier than waterskiing. Rather than having to balance on two skis, you simply kneel on a large board and let the boat pull you along.

WATERSKIING VS. SNOW SKIING

Waterskiing is different from **snow skiing** in several ways. The skis used for waterskiing are wider. You do not usually wear boots while waterskiing because you need to be able to release your feet quickly if you fall in the water. Finally, snow skiers don't need to wear life jackets!

ROCK CLIMBING

ROCK CLIMBING is a fun and challenging sport that can be done outdoors on real rocks or inside on climbing walls. The sport requires good upper body strength because you use your arms to pull yourself up the rocks. Beginners wear a harness designed to catch you if you fall.

WHY CLIMB A MOUNTAIN?

What makes people want to climb mountains? Sir Edmund Hillary, one of the first two men to reach the summit of Mount Everest, is reported to have said, "It is not the mountain we conquer, but ourselves." For more info on Mount Everest, visit: www.mounteverest.net

Indoor rock climbing

Indoor climbing walls have handholds made from rubber or plastic. These allow climbers to hold on as they go up. But what goes up must come down—which is why the harness is important. Once a climber reaches the top, a trained professional holding onto ropes at the bottom guides the climber safely down again.

Hiking and hill climbing

Like rock climbing, hiking and **hill climbing** take place on hills and mountains, but they work your leg muscles more than your arm muscles.

◀ *Rock climbers wear a padded harness that loops around the waist and legs. Safety ropes attach to the harness.*

Outdoor rock climbing

On outdoor rock faces, there are usually no artificial handholds to help you up. Instead, climbers must grip cracks and ledges in the rock. Special shoes provide extra grip.

MOUNTAINEERING

The most extreme version of rock climbing and hiking is called **mountaineering**. Every year, hundreds of people attempt to climb the world's tallest mountains—Mount Everest (29,028 feet/8,848m) and K2 (28,251 feet/8,611m) in the Himalayas. Because true mountaineering takes climbers into high **altitudes**, where there is less oxygen, climbers usually carry special breathing devices and oxygen tanks.

Rock climbers don't just need to be physically strong. They also need to have a positive mental attitude. Climbers need to stay relaxed and confident because some climbs can take many hours.

HIGH RISKS

Climbing mountains, rockfaces, or ice formations (such as ice walls, ice slopes, or **glaciers**) requires special equipment, including **crampons**, **ice axes**, **nuts**, **cams**, and ropes. It should only be done by highly trained professionals who know their equipment, are familiar with the territory, and understand the risks involved.

IF YOU like the water, kayaking may be the extreme sport for you. A kayak is a lightweight, enclosed boat that is paddled on lakes, rivers, or in the ocean. To move the boat, you dip a two-sided paddle into the water on each side of the kayak, one side at a time. Some kayaks are designed for one person, others for two.

LIFE JACKETS

Many states require children to wear life jackets whenever they are in a boat. Life jackets are just as important as seat belts, so don't leave home without one!

Splashing around!

Kayaking is closely related to **canoeing** and **rafting**, both of which are fun boating sports. In the US and Canada, as well as parts of South America and New Zealand, small boats called Sunfish are popular. In the UK, people enjoy sailing and racing Toppers—small, single-person sailing boats.

Sunfish are great sailing boats for children because they're lightweight and easy for one person to sail alone.

KAYAKING

White water kayaking

The most extreme version of kayaking is white water kayaking. You need to be highly trained for this sport. The kayak gets maneuvered through rough and unpredictable "white water" **rapids**, which are very fast flowing. The sport is exciting (even scary) to watch because it can be dangerous. It is definitely not for beginners!

WHITE WATER RAFTING

The most extreme version of rafting is called white water rafting. It requires a trained instructor, a large **inflatable boat**, and a group of friends. The aim is to paddle the boat along a fast-flowing river. Everyone wears life jackets and helmets in case they fall out of the raft.

White water kayakers can choose the difficulty of the river in which they kayak. A Class VI (six) river is the most difficult and dangerous to navigate. A Class I (one) is the easiest.

MULTI-SPORT EVENTS

MULTI-SPORT events are just what they sound like: sporting events that combine multiple sports. There are many different types of multi-sport events. A "triathlon" combines swimming, cycling, and running. ("Tri" is from the Greek word for three.) The winter sport of "biathlon" combines cross-country skiing and rifle shooting (although the term "biathlon" can be used to describe any two-sport event). In a "duathlon," an athlete runs, bikes, and then runs again.

TRIATHLON WORLD CHAMPION

Tim Don of the UK won the men's elite division of the 2006 triathlon World Championships. Don finished the 0.9-mile (1.5km) swim, 24.9-mile (40km) bike ride, and a 6.2-mile (10km) run in 1 hour, 51 minutes, and 32 seconds.

➡ The swimming part of a junior triathlon can take place in a lake or in a pool.

All-around skills

You may be good at swimming, biking, and running, but triathlon requires another skill, too. A triathlete must also be able to change clothes and/or equipment quickly and efficiently at "transitions"—the time between stages. Triathletes need three sets of equipment: goggles and cap for swimming; bike and helmet for biking; and sneakers for running. Keeping it all organized is very important because the quicker the transition time, the faster the finishing time!

TRANSITION AREA

The transition area is the place to which the athlete returns after each leg of the triathlon. After swimming, for instance, the competitor must take off his or her goggles and cap and quickly put on cycling shorts, gloves, shoes, and a helmet.

➡ *After finishing the swim, triathletes run to their bikes, where they put on shoes and a helmet before cycling off.*

➡ *Some athletes wear special suits for all three stages of a triathlon.*

27

Sail and run

Multi-sport events take many different forms. In the UK, the Three Peaks Yacht Race combines yachting (389 miles/626km) and mountain running (72 miles/115.8km), plus a little cycling (18.6 miles/30km). Competitors sail from Barmouth in west Wales to Fort William in northwest Scotland. On the way, they climb to the summits of Britain's three highest peaks: Snowdon, Scafell Pike, and Ben Nevis.

Choice of events

Each year in Oklahoma, competitors can compete in an event called a half REDMAN (swim 1.2 mi/1.9km, bike 56 mi/90km, and run 13 mi/21km); a full REDMAN, which is twice as far— the distance of a full **marathon**); or do the Aqua Bike event (swimming and cycling).

KID STAR

Sara McLarty has been the US IronKids champion four times. She lives in Colorado Springs, Colorado, where the Olympic triathlon team trains. Sara first became an IronKids champion at the age of 10.

➡ *Before attempting the swimming portion of the race, many triathletes do some warm-up exercises and then stretch their arms to give their muscles greater flexibility.*

BODY MARKINGS

Multi-sport competitors are given a number that is marked on their bodies (with permanent ink), attached to their bikes, and pinned to the fronts of their shirts.

The run is sometimes the hardest part of a triathlon because competitors' bodies are already tired from the biking and swimming portions.

Strong as iron!

One of the most famous triathlon events is called the Ironman (in which women also compete). Competitors in this grueling event swim, bike, and run the same distances as a full REDMAN. Children can compete in their own version of the race called IronKids. Junior triathlon distances might include a 137-yard (125m) swim, a 4.9-mile (8km) bike ride, and a 1.6-mile (2.5km) run.

GLOSSARY

altitude The height of a landmass or mountain above sea level.

bicycle motocross (BMX) A sport in which special mountain bikes are raced over rough ground around a hilly course.

box kite A classic type of kite in the shape of a rectangular box.

caliper brakes A type of bicycle brake found on road bikes. Caliper brakes attach above the wheel and squeeze together on either side of the wheel rim to slow the bike down.

cams (mountaineering) Cams are grooved, wheel-like devices with handles. They are inserted into cracks in the rock and attached to climbing ropes. If placed at frequent intervals up the rockface, they will stop a climber from falling very far.

canoeing Paddling a canoe—a long, narrow boat with pointed ends like a kayak, but with an open top.

cantilever brakes A type of bicycle brake found on mountain bikes. Cantilever brakes attach next to the wheel and are more powerful than caliper brakes.

coach Someone who trains or instructs an individual or a team in a particular sport and helps them to improve their skills.

crampon An iron plate with spikes that gets attached to boots to give grip when walking on ice.

glacier A large body of ice moving very slowly down a valley.

Gravity Games An annual competition for extreme sporting events, such as snowboarding.

hiking To walk, climb, explore, and/or travel along paths and trails. Hiking trails are often found in places such as mountainous areas, forests, and along the coast.

hill climbing To climb or hike up hills, sometimes holding long poles for support.

ice ax An ax used by mountaineers for cutting footholds in the ice. One end is hooked and has a serrated edge (like a steak knife).

inflatable boat A boat that is filled with air in order to float.

marathon A road race covering a distance of 26.2 miles (42.2km).

motocross A sport in which a motorcycle is raced over rough or hilly terrain.

mountaineering The sport of walking, hiking, and rock climbing mountains, often over snow and ice. It is also known as Alpinism, particularly in Europe.

nuts (mountaineering) Metal wedges that can be inserted into cracks in the rock, and to which ropes are attached, to stop a climber from falling very far.

oxygen tank A tank that holds oxygen and is used when swimming underwater or mountaineering in high altitudes.

rafting To ride an inflatable raft down a river, often over rapids.

rapids Fast-moving parts of a river, where the water tumbles over and between rocks. Rapids are also known as "white water" because the bubbles make the water look white.

resin A liquid substance that hardens; artificial resins are used in some plastics. Natural resin is found in the gum of some trees.

scuba The letters "scuba" stand for Self Contained Underwater Breathing Apparatus. It is the name given to part of the gear used by underwater divers.

skimmer A round, thin board with no fin. It is about half the length and thickness of a surfboard.

slalom To move in a zigzag formation between obstacles.

snow skiing A sport in which participants use a pair of skis to glide down a snow-covered mountain.

snowboarder Someone who rides a long, flat board down ski slopes or in terrain parks.

snowkiting A sport in which you stand on a snowboard and are pulled along by a kite, which is powered by the wind.

snowmobiling A sport in which you race a motorized sled across ice and snow.

terrain Land used for activities such as mountain biking or hiking.

trail A path used for sports such as walking, hiking, and mountain biking. In snowboarding and snow skiing, the path that takes you from the top of the mountain to the bottom.

triathlon A multi-sport event that combines swimming, biking (road or mountain), and running.

windsurfing A sport that involves standing up on a board similar to a surfboard. A windsurfing board has a sail and moves across the water using the power of the wind.

X Games An international competition similar to the Olympics that includes sports such as skateboarding.

WEB SITES
Mountain biking www.imba.com
Snowkiting www.snowkiting.ch
Waterskiing www.usawaterski.org
Rock climbing (Mount Everest) www.mounteverest.net
General www.guinnessworldrecords. com

Index

INDEX